What Happens Next?

Created by Elle Simms

ISBN-13: 979-8662728424

LET YOUR IMAGINATION

run wild

What is a Story?

Stories tell of events that have happened. These events can be **real** or **imaginary**. They exist to entertain us, to give a particular point of view, or leave us feeling a certain way.

Have you ever read a story that left you thinking about it long after it was over? Good stories are memorable ones. They linger in our minds and sometimes our hearts.

Take a moment to think about your favourite story. What did you like about it? Were you pulled into the world in a way where you could see, hear, smell and taste it? Maybe you never knew what was coming next and it left you on the edge of your seat. Or perhaps you felt as though you knew the characters as if they were real people. These are all characteristics of good storytelling.

Anyone can tell a story, but not everyone can tell a great story. This book will teach you how to write a fantastic (or at least better) story. If you are one of those people who don't enjoy writing, you will find using the outlines in the second part of this book especially helpful.

Basic Elements of a Story

The Idea

This might seem obvious, but all stories start somewhere. Ideas can come from our own experiences or from our imagination. If you are stuck for an idea, try asking **what if...?**

When you ask **what if**, anything is possible.

Two Kinds of Stories

Writing falls into two general categories:

▷ **Fiction:** Made up or imaginary tales. Some examples of fiction are books like the *Harry Potter* series or *Charlotte's Web*, as well as pretend diaries such as *Diary of a Wimpy Kid*. Most stories we read are fiction. Even when they seem like they totally could have happened, they never actually did.

▷ **Nonfiction:** Facts or events that really did happen. Some examples of nonfiction writing are the graphic novel *Smile*, real diaries like *Anne Frank - The Diary of a Young Girl*, cookbooks, most essays, and textbooks. True crime novels and biographies are examples of popular nonfiction stories. Although there are many nonfiction stories available, the vast majority you will find will be fiction.

What kind of writing do you prefer?

☐ Fiction   or   ☐ Nonfiction

For most people, writing fiction is easier than writing nonfiction. Nonfiction writing requires sticking to the facts which might require research. Plus, it can be a challenge to turn facts into an exciting story. It is for that reason, that the ideas given in the second part of this book are fiction focused. There are a few blank outlines also included, which you can use for any nonfiction ideas you might have.

Developing a Story

Have you ever had a great idea for a story, but did not finish writing it because you couldn't figure out how to get to the end? Planning is an important part of writing a story. It might sound like an odd thing to do, because it takes a bit of the excitement out of starting. However, if you take the time to create an outline before you begin to write, you will know how to get from the beginning to the end, without getting stuck.

If you are considering nonfiction, you should have a good idea of who the characters are, how the story ends, and the key points that happen throughout. Should you still take the the time to develop your story?

Yes! There may be some elements you have not thought to include. More importantly, there are ways to shape all those pieces into an engaging tale that will make your audience want to continue reading to the end. Otherwise, it might end up a bit blah... a list of then this happened, then this happened, then this happened, etc.

▷ Characters

These are the people (or animals) in your story. Before you begin writing, you should know your main characters well. What kind of people are they? What do they like and dislike? What are their goals? Their fears? Just as in real life, characters should not be perfect. They should have flaws, doubts, and make mistakes occasionally. This helps the reader relate to them better. Your **protagonist** - your leading character, especially, should be someone that the reader understands and connects with. And, just as in real life, the bad guys in your story should always have at least some small good thing about them. Perhaps they love their cat or tell really funny jokes.

Peter McKnight

Strong, brave and loyal. Loves jousting and rescuing princesses. Hates dragons and green beans. Takes quests very seriously. Can be overconfident.

Sample Character Descriptions

Princess Penelope

Kind-hearted, sweet, and trusting... sometimes too trusting. Has a tendency to wind up in dangerous situations that she can't get herself out of. Loves dwarfs and comfy beds piled high with mattresses. Has many animal friends and sings a lot.

Dudley the Dragon

Ill-tempered and greedy. Attracted to shiny objects. Has superb flying skills and some seriously bad breath. Wanted for crimes of arson.

When describing characters it is natural to want to detail every aspect of what they look like. But relying too much on physical characteristics can be boring.

> BORING: Jared is a boy who is four feet, two inches tall. He has medium length, brown curly hair and hazel eyes. He is wearing blue jeans, an orange t-shirt, white sneakers and a green backpack. He is standing under a tree and he looks sad.

This description of Jared might give you a good idea of what he looks like, but it's not very exciting, and it doesn't tell us what he is thinking or why he feels the way that he does.

> BETTER: Jared's small frame slumped under the weight of his backpack, as he waited under the maple tree. Brushing his curly hair out of his eyes, he thought about the fight he'd had with his best friend, wishing he could take back the things he had said.

This description contains less of Jared's physical description, yet we are able to understand his character a little better. It illustrates both how he feels and why he feels that way.

This doesn't mean that we shouldn't describe what a person looks like. Go ahead, but try to pick the traits that stand out the most, or that are important to the story. The reader will fill the rest in with their imagination.

The following are some ways to describe characters besides their appearance:

- **Personality:** Are they stubborn? Dependable? Creative? Generous?

- **Habits:** Do they twirl their hair? Pick their nose? Tap their toes? Bite their lip when they are thinking?

- **Beliefs:** Do they believe in leprechauns? Are they a dedicated vegan? Do they believe that love conquers all? Are they certain they will be famous someday?

- **Strengths:** Are they a mathematical genius? Do they have a superpower? Perhaps they put 100% effort into everything they do. Or are able to convince others to do things they dont want to. Maybe they're just a really nice person.

- **Weaknesses:** Nobody is perfect. Is your character a klutz? Do they daydream too much? Have terrible allergies? Are they always saying the wrong thing?

- **Fears:** What does your character fear most? Is it losing a loved one? Being humiliated? Are they agoraphobic? Afraid of spiders?

- **Quirks:** In what small way is your character weird or different than other people? Does your character have an eye that twitches when they are angry? Do they sing all the time, but horribly?

A character's traits should match the choices they make in your story. For example, an honest person would not tell a lie. When a character goes against what they normally would do in a situation, there should be a good reason. For example, a normally honest person might lie to protect a person they love, but it might take extraordinary circumstances.

Though she knew it was wrong, Arianna lied about being with Maddy that night. She couldn't bear the thought of Maddy being blamed for something she didn't do.

▷ Setting

The setting of your story is where it all happens. It may take place in multiple places (home, school, park). When establishing the setting try to describe it using all of your senses. Describe what your characters see, smell and hear. You don't have to put in every detail of a room or aspect of the weather. The reader's imagination will fill in the small gaps. Simply try to paint a clear but basic picture in the reader's mind of the environment surrounding the characters.

Here are a few things to take into consideration when writing about the setting:

- **Location:** Where is the story currently taking place? A messy bedroom? An amusement park? A remote space station on a dry and barren planet?

- **Time:** When does the story take place? Is it happening now, in modern times? Maybe it is happening in the future, or ten years ago, or the time of the dinosaurs. Your story may be a fantasy, and takes place in a kingdom that never really existed and a time that never was, the way that *The Hobbit* takes place in Middle Earth. Does your world have a history? What time of day is it? What season?

- **Use your Senses:** What do you see? Smell? Hear? Do you smell the saltiness of the ocean? And hear the deafening roar of waves crashing onto a beach?

- **Mood:** What does it feel like to be there? Does the smell of cookies baking make you feel right at home? Do dusty cobwebs and creaking floorboards give you the creeps?

▷ Inciting Incident

This happens at the the beginning of a story. It often comes in the form of a problem that the lead character must deal with. And it is the event that causes the rest of the story to unfold. The inciting incident should grab the reader's attention, making them wonder what will come next.

> Henry and his mother sat across from Principal Banner. Mom's cheeks were flushed and she clutched her purse too tightly.
>
> This whole mess had started with a simple paperclip. That's what Henry had been looking for when he was rummaging around in Mrs. Jackson's drawer. He never meant to find the answers to tomorrow's science test. Why wouldn't they believe him?

In the second part of this book you will find more than thirty inciting incidents you can use to create stories.

▶ Plot

The plot is the series of events that your characters go through from beginning to end. Each event should be essential to the story. This is why characters rarely talk about the the weather. The action and excitement should build to a climax.

1. **Exposition:** The exposition of a story includes the basic elements that we have just covered like the setting, main characters, and the inciting incident. It gives information that the reader should know before diving into the story.

2. **Rising Action:** The rising action is the series of events that build tension, conflict and suspense. These events lead to the point of highest tension or suspense.

3. **Climax:** The climax is the highest point of adventure or excitement in your story. It is when, for example, the hero is about to save the world, or detective finds the final clue, or when the team needs just one more point to win the championship and there is only seconds left to play. It may simply be a character about to solve their problem after a series of hardships or failures.

4. **Resolution:** The problem from the inciting incident is resolved, or a goal is achieved, and the story comes to an end. For example, the world is saved, the mystery solved, or the team wins the game.

5. **Denouement:** This is anything that happens after the resolution. Any loose ends are wrapped up and the story comes to an end. What happens afterward?

Plotting the major elements of your story before you begin writing will help you stay focused on what comes next and how to get there. This is called an **outline**.

Climax
The highest point of excitement.

Rising Action
The series of events that lead to the climax.

Resolution
The problem is solved or goal is reached.

Exposition & Inciting Incident
The background, and introduction to main characters and problem/goal.

Denouement
Where the end of the story wraps up.

Plotting a Story

For Example...

Exposition: Things have been going missing around the sleepy town of Boringville where twelve year old Ben lives.

Inciting Incident: When his bike disappears, Ben decides to solve the mystery.

Rising Action:
1. Ben questions neighbours.
2. He finds a suspect.
3. Ben sets up a trap to catch the thief.

Climax: The thief nearly escapes.

Resolution: Ben catches the thief.

Denouement: Ben is a hero. The mayor of Boringville awards Ben a medal for his efforts.

▷ Point of View

Who is telling your story? Every story has a narrator. Although you are the writer, your story may be told from someone else's perspective.

We use different terms for describing point of view:

Point of View	Voice	Uses Words Like	Example
FIRST PERSON	Someone who is a character in the story.	I, Me, My (I reached for the wand.)	-*Wonder* -*The One and Only Ivan* -*Junie B. Jones* series
SECOND PERSON	Puts the reader into the story.	You, Your (You reach for the wand.)	-*Choose Your Own Adventure* series -*You Wouldn't Want To* series
THIRD PERSON	Story is about something that happened to someone else	He/She, His/Her (He reached for the wand.)	-*The Lion, the Witch and the Wardrobe* -*Coraline*

Point of view also depicts **when** the story happens, whether it is happening in the past, present or future.

- PAST: Alicia picked up the medallion.
- PRESENT: Alicia picks up the medallion.
- FUTURE: Alicia will pick up the medallion.

As you can probably guess, from the examples above, stories are nearly always told in past or present tense.

Unless you are writing a very long story, you should keep the same point of view throughout. There are exceptions. Some stories are told through the eyes of multiple characters, or go back and forth in time. This is probably more appropriate for a novel, where different viewpoints can be separated into chapters. For a shorter story, it will be confusing for the reader.

▷ Conflict

All good stories have conflict. Conflicts are struggles that keep your characters from achieving their goals or solving their problems. It creates suspense and drama. Conflicts can be internal or external.

- **Internal:** Conflict comes from WITHIN the character.

> Jessa waited outside the principal's office. Her stomach churned. It would be so easy to lie, and blame it on Quinn, she thought.

- **External:** Conflict comes from OUTSIDE the character.

> Quinn smirked at Jessa. "I'm going to tell them it was all your fault!"

▷ Theme

Many stories have meanings or messages. Though they may not be directly stated in the story, it is implied through the actions and thoughts of the characters, how they deal with their problems and what they learn from them. Themes are often universal. This means that people everywhere can recognize and relate to them.

Some common themes in stories are:

- love can conquer all
- good triumphs over evil
- you can find happiness after loss
- hard work brings reward
- the importance of friendship
- the truth will set you free

You may have heard these things said before but may not have realized that these themes exist in stories. You don't need to incorporate a theme into every story that you write, but doing so will make your story more powerful.

▷ Tone

Tone is the feeling that comes through in what you are writing. Try saying the following sentence, out loud, using two different tones - one peaceful and one frightening.

> The boy stood, alone, in a thicket of apsen trees.

Do you see how the same information might mean very different things?

The best way to convey tone in writing is through our choice of words. It isn't so much what you say, but how you choose to say it. For instance, these two sentences convey the same basic information in two entirely different ways.

> The ghostly moon cast a pale light over the sleeping town below, sneaking through windows, to settle on unsuspecting villagers.

> The bright light of the moon illuminated the town below, shining through windows to warm the faces of the sleeping villagers.

Choosing the right words can make a huge difference in the tone of your story. If you get stuck trying to find the right word, try using a thesaurus.

▷ Show, Don't Tell

This is one of the most important rules in story telling. It means that instead of telling the reader what happens, we demonstrate it instead. Showing what happens paints a clearer picture in the mind of the reader.

> TELLING: Jack was nervous.
> SHOWING: Jack's palms were sweaty and his stomach was in knots.
>
> TELLING: It snowed.
> SHOWING: Soft, white flakes drifted down from pillowy clouds.
>
> TELLING: Sophie liked the ice cream.
> SHOWING: Sophie licked her fudge brownie cone slowly, savouring every mouthful.
>
> TELLING: The dog looked mean.
> SHOWING: The beast's nostrils flared and it's lip curled into a viscious snarl. It pawed at the ground, threatening to break the thin metal chain.

Story Ideas

Ideas for stories can come from anywhere. You might find inspiration in real life - events that actually happened, or from something you read in a book, or saw in a movie. They can come from your dreams or just popped into your head out of nowhere one day.

Whether your story is true or imaginary, it is helpful to create an outline before you begin writing it down.

In this section you will find more than thirty story ideas with a templates for outlining them. At the very back are a few blank templates, in case you prefer to use one of your own.

These story prompts/inciting incidents are written as though they happened to you. And you may write them that way, in first person, past tense. However, if you would prefer to create a fictional protagonist, or change some other aspect, please do. Most details have been left out so that you can use your imagination and make the story your very own. Also, they are not meant to be the first few sentences of a story, just an idea. You should rewrite it, in your own unique style. This will give you the opportunity to add detail, establish a setting, etc.

Lastly, don't forget to have fun with the ideas! It's okay if your story isn't perfect, or you can't find a way to incorporate a theme or some other aspect. Story telling and writing are both things that improve over time.

Time to get your imagination running…

Name of Story: _____

IDEA / INCITING INCIDENT:

You wake up in the middle of the night to discover that you are floating above your bed.

SETTING Describe three different aspects of the setting.

- _____
- _____
- _____

CHARACTERS: List three characters. Describe each character in three ways. Put a star beside the protagonist's (leading character's) name.

1 _____
  NAME

- _____
- _____
- _____

2 _____
  NAME

- _____
- _____
- _____

3 _____
  NAME

- _____
- _____

From whose point of view will the story be told? _____

When does the story take place? _____

What is the tone of your story?

Does your story have a theme?

RISING ACTION: Write down your major plot points.

1

2

3

4

5

6

7

CLIMAX: What is the highest point of excitement in your story?

RESOLUTION: What is the outcome?

DENOUMENT: Wrap up your loose ends.

Name of Story: _____

IDEA / INCITING INCIDENT:

You are hiking with your dog when he sniffs out a strange nest containing a solitary egg the size of a football. It is unlike any egg you have ever seen before. You gently pick it up to examine it more closely and hear something scratching inside.

SETTING Describe three different aspects of the setting.

- _____
- _____
- _____

CHARACTERS: List three characters. Describe each character in three ways. Put a star beside the protagonist's (leading character's) name.

1 _____
     NAME
- _____
- _____
- _____

2 _____
     NAME
- _____
- _____
- _____

3 _____
     NAME
- _____
- _____

From whose point of view will the story be told? _____

When does the story take place? _____

What is the tone of your story? _____

Does your story have a theme? _____

RISING ACTION: Write down your major plot points.

1 _____

2 _____

3 _____

4 _____

5 _____

6 _____

7 _____

CLIMAX: What is the highest point of excitement in your story?

_____

RESOLUTION: What is the outcome?

_____

DENOUMENT: Wrap up your loose ends.

_____

Name of Story: _____

IDEA / INCITING INCIDENT:

Your class is visiting a museum. A bully, who is always picking on you, smashes the case of a priceless artifact. Sirens go off and lights flash. He reaches in and tosses the artifact to you. You are still holding it when security guards come rushing in. "Thief!" the bully shouts, pointing in your direction.

SETTING Describe three different aspects of the setting.

- _____
- _____
- _____

CHARACTERS: List three characters. Describe each character in three ways. Put a star beside the protagonist's (leading character's) name.

1 _____
　　　NAME
- _____
- _____
- _____

2 _____
　　　NAME
- _____
- _____
- _____

3 _____
　　　NAME
- _____
- _____

From whose point of view will the story be told? _____

When does the story take place? _____

What is the tone of your story? _____

Does your story have a theme? _____

RISING ACTION: Write down your major plot points.

1 _____

2 _____

3 _____

4 _____

5 _____

6 _____

7 _____

CLIMAX: What is the highest point of excitement in your story?

_____

RESOLUTION: What is the outcome?

_____

DENOUMENT: Wrap up your loose ends.

_____

Name of Story: _____

IDEA / INCITING INCIDENT:

You are part of a crew exploring the far reaches of the galaxy. You have been wandering around an unknown planet that has dense vegetation but no animals or higher life forms. At least that's what you thought... until you ran into the angry, three-eyed, foul smelling creature before you. You are armed only with plastic sample bags and tweezers.

SETTING Describe three different aspects of the setting.

- _____
- _____
- _____

CHARACTERS: List three characters. Describe each character in three ways. Put a star beside the protagonist's (leading character's) name.

1 _____
    NAME

- _____
- _____
- _____

2 _____
    NAME

- _____
- _____
- _____

3 _____
    NAME

- _____
- _____

From whose point of view will the story be told? _____

When does the story take place? _____

What is the tone of your story? _____

Does your story have a theme? _____

RISING ACTION: Write down your major plot points.

1 _____

2 _____

3 _____

4 _____

5 _____

6 _____

7 _____

CLIMAX: What is the highest point of excitement in your story?

_____

RESOLUTION: What is the outcome?

_____

DENOUMENT: Wrap up your loose ends.

_____

Name of Story: _____

IDEA / INCITING INCIDENT:

One day you discover that if you concentrate hard enough, you can read the minds... of cats. What is more remarkable is that you realize they are planning to take over the world and make humans their slaves.

SETTING Describe three different aspects of the setting.

- _____
- _____
- _____

CHARACTERS: List three characters. Describe each character in three ways. Put a star beside the protagonist's (leading character's) name.

1 _____
NAME
- _____
- _____
- _____

2 _____
NAME
- _____
- _____
- _____

3 _____
NAME
- _____
- _____

From whose point of view will the story be told? _____

When does the story take place? _____

What is the tone of your story? _____

Does your story have a theme? _____

RISING ACTION: Write down your major plot points.

1 _____

2 _____

3 _____

4 _____

5 _____

6 _____

7 _____

CLIMAX: What is the highest point of excitement in your story?

_____

RESOLUTION: What is the outcome?

_____

DENOUMENT: Wrap up your loose ends.

_____

Name of Story: _____

IDEA / INCITING INCIDENT:

As you are walking down the street one day, a terrified looking man begs you for help. "Pray help me. I beg thou!" You can't help but notice that he speaks with an accent and is dressed in medieval armor. As a car drives by he dives into the bushes, pulling you with him. "Where am I? What is this magical place?"

SETTING Describe three different aspects of the setting.

- _____
- _____
- _____

CHARACTERS: List three characters. Describe each character in three ways. Put a star beside the protagonist's (leading character's) name.

1 _____
    NAME
- _____
- _____
- _____

2 _____
    NAME
- _____
- _____
- _____

3 _____
    NAME
- _____
- _____

From whose point of view will the story be told? _____

When does the story take place? _____

What is the tone of your story? _____

Does your story have a theme? _____

RISING ACTION: Write down your major plot points.

1 _____

2 _____

3 _____

4 _____

5 _____

6 _____

7 _____

CLIMAX: What is the highest point of excitement in your story?

_____

RESOLUTION: What is the outcome?

_____

DENOUMENT: Wrap up your loose ends.

_____

Name of Story: _____

IDEA / INCITING INCIDENT:

While looking for a missing item, you discover a drawer with a false bottom. When you open it, you find thirty thousand dollars, passports with your family's photos (but with different names), and a letter written in code. Your Mom walks in to find you holding it all. "You weren't supposed to know about that," she says.

SETTING Describe three different aspects of the setting.

- _____
- _____
- _____

CHARACTERS: List three characters. Describe each character in three ways. Put a star beside the protagonist's (leading character's) name.

1 _____
    NAME
- _____
- _____
- _____

2 _____
    NAME
- _____
- _____
- _____

3 _____
    NAME
- _____
- _____

From whose point of view will the story be told? _____

When does the story take place? _____

What is the tone of your story?

_____

Does your story have a theme?

_____

RISING ACTION: Write down your major plot points.

1 _____

2 _____

3 _____

4 _____

5 _____

6 _____

7 _____

CLIMAX: What is the highest point of excitement in your story?

_____

RESOLUTION: What is the outcome?

_____

DENOUMENT: Wrap up your loose ends.

_____

Name of Story: _____

IDEA / INCITING INCIDENT:

A time machine has just been invented and you have been randomly chosen through a national lottery to be its first
test subject.

SETTING Describe three different aspects of the setting.

- _____
- _____
- _____

CHARACTERS: List three characters. Describe each character in three ways. Put a star beside the
protagonist's (leading character's) name.

1 _____
     NAME
- _____
- _____
- _____

2 _____
     NAME
- _____
- _____
- _____

3 _____
     NAME
- _____
- _____

From whose point of view will the story be told? _____

When does the story take place? _____

What is the tone of your story? _____

Does your story have a theme? _____

RISING ACTION: Write down your major plot points.

1 _____

2 _____

3 _____

4 _____

5 _____

6 _____

7 _____

CLIMAX: What is the highest point of excitement in your story?

_____

RESOLUTION: What is the outcome?

_____

DENOUMENT: Wrap up your loose ends.

_____

Name of Story: _____

IDEA / INCITING INCIDENT:

You are camping in the woods and hear strange noises in the night. You unzip the door flap and see something utterly terrifying.

SETTING Describe three different aspects of the setting.

- _____
- _____
- _____

CHARACTERS: List three characters. Describe each character in three ways. Put a star beside the protagonist's (leading character's) name.

1 _____
   NAME
- _____
- _____
- _____

2 _____
   NAME
- _____
- _____
- _____

3 _____
   NAME
- _____
- _____

From whose point of view will the story be told? _____

When does the story take place? _____

What is the tone of your story?

Does your story have a theme?

RISING ACTION: Write down your major plot points.

1

2

3

4

5

6

7

CLIMAX: What is the highest point of excitement in your story?

RESOLUTION: What is the outcome?

DENOUMENT: Wrap up your loose ends.

Name of Story: _____

IDEA / INCITING INCIDENT:

All around you, electrical appliances start acting strangely. Toasters pop, televisions switch stations and lights flicker on and off. Wherever you go, your presence has an effect on things that use electricity.

SETTING Describe three different aspects of the setting.

- _____
- _____
- _____

CHARACTERS: List three characters. Describe each character in three ways. Put a star beside the protagonist's (leading character's) name.

1 _____
  NAME
- _____
- _____
- _____

2 _____
  NAME
- _____
- _____
- _____

3 _____
  NAME
- _____
- _____

From whose point of view will the story be told? _____

When does the story take place? _____

What is the tone of your story? _____

Does your story have a theme? _____

RISING ACTION: Write down your major plot points.

1 _____

2 _____

3 _____

4 _____

5 _____

6 _____

7 _____

CLIMAX: What is the highest point of excitement in your story?

_____

RESOLUTION: What is the outcome?

_____

DENOUMENT: Wrap up your loose ends.

_____

Name of Story: _____

IDEA / INCITING INCIDENT:

Your parents mysteriously vanish, leaving a note that says not to tell anyone, and that they should be back in one month. They have left YOU in charge.

SETTING Describe three different aspects of the setting.

- _____
- _____
- _____

CHARACTERS: List three characters. Describe each character in three ways. Put a star beside the protagonist's (leading character's) name.

1 _____
   NAME
- _____
- _____
- _____

2 _____
   NAME
- _____
- _____
- _____

3 _____
   NAME
- _____
- _____

From whose point of view will the story be told? _____

When does the story take place? _____

What is the tone of your story? _____

Does your story have a theme? _____

RISING ACTION: Write down your major plot points.

1 _____

2 _____

3 _____

4 _____

5 _____

6 _____

7 _____

CLIMAX: What is the highest point of excitement in your story?

_____

RESOLUTION: What is the outcome?

_____

DENOUMENT: Wrap up your loose ends.

_____

Name of Story: _____

IDEA / INCITING INCIDENT:

You just downloaded a block world game. You set it to survival mode and put it on hard because you want a challenge. When you press start, you are sucked into the game for real. There is nothing in your inventory and you have only eight minutes before day turns into night and the monsters come out.

SETTING Describe three different aspects of the setting.

- _____
- _____
- _____

CHARACTERS: List three characters. Describe each character in three ways. Put a star beside the protagonist's (leading character's) name.

1 _____
    NAME
- _____
- _____
- _____

2 _____
    NAME
- _____
- _____
- _____

3 _____
    NAME
- _____
- _____

From whose point of view will the story be told? _____

When does the story take place? _____

What is the tone of your story? _____

Does your story have a theme? _____

RISING ACTION: Write down your major plot points.

1 _____

2 _____

3 _____

4 _____

5 _____

6 _____

7 _____

CLIMAX: What is the highest point of excitement in your story?

_____

RESOLUTION: What is the outcome?

_____

DENOUMENT: Wrap up your loose ends.

_____

Name of Story: _____

IDEA / INCITING INCIDENT:

You answer the door and see balloons, streamers, camera crew, and a man with a microphone. "You've just won ten million dollars!" He hands you a giant check with your name on it.

SETTING Describe three different aspects of the setting.

- _____
- _____
- _____

CHARACTERS: List three characters. Describe each character in three ways. Put a star beside the protagonist's (leading character's) name.

1 _____
    NAME
- _____
- _____
- _____

2 _____
    NAME
- _____
- _____
- _____

3 _____
    NAME
- _____
- _____

From whose point of view will the story be told? _____

When does the story take place? _____

What is the tone of your story? _____

Does your story have a theme? _____

RISING ACTION: Write down your major plot points.

1 _____

2 _____

3 _____

4 _____

5 _____

6 _____

7 _____

CLIMAX: What is the highest point of excitement in your story?

_____

RESOLUTION: What is the outcome?

_____

DENOUMENT: Wrap up your loose ends.

_____

Name of Story: _____

IDEA / INCITING INCIDENT:

You moved into a new house today and your room has a mouse sized door at the base of one wall. You assume it is just a decoration left by the kid who used to live there. As you fall asleep that night you hear strange sounds coming from behind it and see a glimmer of light shining around the edges.

SETTING Describe three different aspects of the setting.

- _____
- _____
- _____

CHARACTERS: List three characters. Describe each character in three ways. Put a star beside the protagonist's (leading character's) name.

1 _____
　　　　NAME
- _____
- _____
- _____

2 _____
　　　　NAME
- _____
- _____
- _____

3 _____
　　　　NAME
- _____
- _____

From whose point of view will the story be told? _____

When does the story take place? _____

What is the tone of your story? _____

Does your story have a theme? _____

RISING ACTION: Write down your major plot points.

1 _____

2 _____

3 _____

4 _____

5 _____

6 _____

7 _____

CLIMAX: What is the highest point of excitement in your story?

_____

RESOLUTION: What is the outcome?

_____

DENOUMENT: Wrap up your loose ends.

_____

Name of Story: _____

IDEA / INCITING INCIDENT:

You are competing in a real life room escape game. You find the key, open the door and step out into a... cage? The door slams shut behind you. There is nowhere to go. Is this part of the game, you wonder. A deep voice says, "We got another one, Frank." You look around but don't see anyone. Suddenly, the cage you are in is hoisted into the air.

SETTING Describe three different aspects of the setting.

- _____
- _____
- _____

CHARACTERS: List three characters. Describe each character in three ways. Put a star beside the protagonist's (leading character's) name.

1 _____
    NAME

- _____
- _____
- _____

2 _____
    NAME

- _____
- _____
- _____

3 _____
    NAME

- _____
- _____

From whose point of view will the story be told? _____

When does the story take place? _____

What is the tone of your story?

_____

Does your story have a theme?

_____

RISING ACTION: Write down your major plot points.

1 _____

2 _____

3 _____

4 _____

5 _____

6 _____

7 _____

CLIMAX: What is the highest point of excitement in your story?

_____

RESOLUTION: What is the outcome?

_____

DENOUMENT: Wrap up your loose ends.

_____

Name of Story: _____

IDEA / INCITING INCIDENT:

You wake up in the morning, and scratch behind your ear – with your foot! You look into the mirror and realize you've turned into a dog.

SETTING Describe three different aspects of the setting.

- _____
- _____
- _____

CHARACTERS: List three characters. Describe each character in three ways. Put a star beside the protagonist's (leading character's) name.

1 _____
     NAME

- _____
- _____
- _____

2 _____
     NAME

- _____
- _____
- _____

3 _____
     NAME

- _____
- _____

From whose point of view will the story be told? _____

When does the story take place? _____

What is the tone of your story? _____

Does your story have a theme? _____

RISING ACTION: Write down your major plot points.

1 _____

2 _____

3 _____

4 _____

5 _____

6 _____

7 _____

CLIMAX: What is the highest point of excitement in your story?

_____

RESOLUTION: What is the outcome?

_____

DENOUMENT: Wrap up your loose ends.

_____

Name of Story: _____

IDEA / INCITING INCIDENT:

You get hit by lightning and are suddenly amazingly good at the one thing you could never do well before.

SETTING Describe three different aspects of the setting.

- _____
- _____
- _____

CHARACTERS: List three characters. Describe each character in three ways. Put a star beside the protagonist's (leading character's) name.

1 _____
    NAME
- _____
- _____
- _____

2 _____
    NAME
- _____
- _____
- _____

3 _____
    NAME
- _____
- _____

From whose point of view will the story be told? _____

When does the story take place? _____

What is the tone of your story? _____

Does your story have a theme? _____

RISING ACTION: Write down your major plot points.

1 _____

2 _____

3 _____

4 _____

5 _____

6 _____

7 _____

CLIMAX: What is the highest point of excitement in your story?

_____

RESOLUTION: What is the outcome?

_____

DENOUMENT: Wrap up your loose ends.

_____

Name of Story: _____

IDEA / INCITING INCIDENT:

You spot a bottle of what you think is your favorite drink in the fridge. You can't resist and down the whole thing before you realize it doesn't taste right. You look at the bottle to see what you drank. The label says "Love Potion – WARNING: Do not drink more than one tablespoon per day." Love potions can't be real, you think.

SETTING Describe three different aspects of the setting.

- _____
- _____
- _____

CHARACTERS: List three characters. Describe each character in three ways. Put a star beside the protagonist's (leading character's) name.

1 _____
     NAME

- _____
- _____
- _____

2 _____
     NAME

- _____
- _____
- _____

3 _____
     NAME

- _____
- _____

From whose point of view will the story be told? _____

When does the story take place? _____

What is the tone of your story? _____

Does your story have a theme? _____

RISING ACTION: Write down your major plot points.

1 _____

2 _____

3 _____

4 _____

5 _____

6 _____

7 _____

CLIMAX: What is the highest point of excitement in your story?

_____

RESOLUTION: What is the outcome?

_____

DENOUMENT: Wrap up your loose ends.

_____

Name of Story:

IDEA / INCITING INCIDENT:

Your best friend confides that they are not quite human.

SETTING Describe three different aspects of the setting.

- _____
- _____
- _____

CHARACTERS: List three characters. Describe each character in three ways. Put a star beside the protagonist's (leading character's) name.

1 _____
   NAME
- _____
- _____
- _____

2 _____
   NAME
- _____
- _____
- _____

3 _____
   NAME
- _____
- _____

From whose point of view will the story be told? _____

When does the story take place? _____

What is the tone of your story?

_____

Does your story have a theme?

_____

RISING ACTION: Write down your major plot points.

1 _____

2 _____

3 _____

4 _____

5 _____

6 _____

7 _____

CLIMAX: What is the highest point of excitement in your story?

_____

RESOLUTION: What is the outcome?

_____

DENOUMENT: Wrap up your loose ends.

_____

Name of Story: _____

IDEA / INCITING INCIDENT:

Your beloved pet zombie only listens to your commands and has to be chained up when you're not around. You've just realized that he's missing when you hear news reports of a zombie running amok at the local WallyMart.

SETTING Describe three different aspects of the setting.

- _____
- _____
- _____

CHARACTERS: List three characters. Describe each character in three ways. Put a star beside the protagonist's (leading character's) name.

1 _____
   NAME
- _____
- _____
- _____

2 _____
   NAME
- _____
- _____
- _____

3 _____
   NAME
- _____
- _____

From whose point of view will the story be told? _____

When does the story take place? _____

What is the tone of your story? _____

Does your story have a theme? _____

RISING ACTION: Write down your major plot points.

1 _____

2 _____

3 _____

4 _____

5 _____

6 _____

7 _____

CLIMAX: What is the highest point of excitement in your story?

_____

RESOLUTION: What is the outcome?

_____

DENOUMENT: Wrap up your loose ends.

_____

Name of Story: _____

IDEA / INCITING INCIDENT:

You are attending a live magic show and it's the worst you've ever seen. The tricks are just terrible. Afterword, the magician catches you complaining about it to your friend. "I'll show you magic," he says angrily. He waves his wand over you. You try to apologize for being so rude and find yourself unable to speak at all.

SETTING Describe three different aspects of the setting.

- _____
- _____
- _____

CHARACTERS: List three characters. Describe each character in three ways. Put a star beside the protagonist's (leading character's) name.

1 _____
   NAME
- _____
- _____
- _____

2 _____
   NAME
- _____
- _____
- _____

3 _____
   NAME
- _____
- _____

From whose point of view will the story be told? _____

When does the story take place? _____

What is the tone of your story?

_____

Does your story have a theme?

_____

RISING ACTION: Write down your major plot points.

1 _____

2 _____

3 _____

4 _____

5 _____

6 _____

7 _____

CLIMAX: What is the highest point of excitement in your story?

_____

RESOLUTION: What is the outcome?

_____

DENOUMENT: Wrap up your loose ends.

_____

Name of Story: _____

IDEA / INCITING INCIDENT:

You come home from school one day, and head to your room. When you open the door, there is someone who looks exactly like you sitting on your bed. "Who are you? And what are you doing in my house?" they yell.

SETTING Describe three different aspects of the setting.

- _____
- _____
- _____

CHARACTERS: List three characters. Describe each character in three ways. Put a star beside the protagonist's (leading character's) name.

1 _____
   NAME

- _____
- _____
- _____

2 _____
   NAME

- _____
- _____
- _____

3 _____
   NAME

- _____
- _____

From whose point of view will the story be told? _____

When does the story take place? _____

What is the tone of your story?

Does your story have a theme?

RISING ACTION: Write down your major plot points.

1

2

3

4

5

6

7

CLIMAX: What is the highest point of excitement in your story?

RESOLUTION: What is the outcome?

DENOUMENT: Wrap up your loose ends.

Name of Story: _____

IDEA / INCITING INCIDENT:

An angry army of glow in the dark rats escape from a local laboratory and take over your school. What happens next?

SETTING Describe three different aspects of the setting.

- _____
- _____
- _____

CHARACTERS: List three characters. Describe each character in three ways. Put a star beside the protagonist's (leading character's) name.

1 _____
    NAME

- _____
- _____
- _____

2 _____
    NAME

- _____
- _____
- _____

3 _____
    NAME

- _____
- _____

From whose point of view will the story be told? _____

When does the story take place? _____

What is the tone of your story?

_____

Does your story have a theme?

_____

RISING ACTION: Write down your major plot points.

1 _____

2 _____

3 _____

4 _____

5 _____

6 _____

7 _____

CLIMAX: What is the highest point of excitement in your story?

_____

RESOLUTION: What is the outcome?

_____

DENOUMENT: Wrap up your loose ends.

_____

Name of Story: _____

IDEA / INCITING INCIDENT:

You wake up alone on the shore of a tropical island after your cruise ship goes down in the middle of the South Pacific. You search frantically for other survivors but all you find are some bits of wreckage, a sand filled suitcase, and half a bottle of root beer.

SETTING Describe three different aspects of the setting.

- _____
- _____
- _____

CHARACTERS: List three characters. Describe each character in three ways. Put a star beside the protagonist's (leading character's) name.

1 _____
    NAME
- _____
- _____
- _____

2 _____
    NAME
- _____
- _____
- _____

3 _____
    NAME
- _____
- _____

From whose point of view will the story be told? _____

When does the story take place? _____

What is the tone of your story?

_____

Does your story have a theme?

_____

RISING ACTION: Write down your major plot points.

1 _____

2 _____

3 _____

4 _____

5 _____

6 _____

7 _____

CLIMAX: What is the highest point of excitement in your story?

_____

RESOLUTION: What is the outcome?

_____

DENOUMENT: Wrap up your loose ends.

_____

Name of Story:

IDEA / INCITING INCIDENT:

Your mousetrap accidentally catches a fairy. And it's alive!

SETTING Describe three different aspects of the setting.

-
-
-

CHARACTERS: List three characters. Describe each character in three ways. Put a star beside the protagonist's (leading character's) name.

1 _____
     NAME

-
-
-

2 _____
     NAME

-
-
-

3 _____
     NAME

-
-

From whose point of view will the story be told?

When does the story take place?

What is the tone of your story? _____

Does your story have a theme? _____

RISING ACTION: Write down your major plot points.

1 _____

2 _____

3 _____

4 _____

5 _____

6 _____

7 _____

CLIMAX: What is the highest point of excitement in your story?

_____

RESOLUTION: What is the outcome?

_____

DENOUMENT: Wrap up your loose ends.

_____

Name of Story: _____

IDEA / INCITING INCIDENT:

You have an adverse reaction to the new shampoo your Mom bought. It has caused you to rapidly grow hair over your entire body.

SETTING Describe three different aspects of the setting.

- _____
- _____
- _____

CHARACTERS: List three characters. Describe each character in three ways. Put a star beside the protagonist's (leading character's) name.

1 _____
    NAME

- _____
- _____
- _____

2 _____
    NAME

- _____
- _____
- _____

3 _____
    NAME

- _____
- _____

From whose point of view will the story be told? _____

When does the story take place? _____

What is the tone of your story? _____

Does your story have a theme? _____

RISING ACTION: Write down your major plot points.

1 _____

2 _____

3 _____

4 _____

5 _____

6 _____

7 _____

CLIMAX: What is the highest point of excitement in your story?

_____

RESOLUTION: What is the outcome?

_____

DENOUMENT: Wrap up your loose ends.

_____

Name of Story: _____

IDEA / INCITING INCIDENT:

Your parents sit you down to have a serious discussion. "It's time you knew," they tell you.

SETTING Describe three different aspects of the setting.

- _____
- _____
- _____

CHARACTERS: List three characters. Describe each character in three ways. Put a star beside the protagonist's (leading character's) name.

1 _____
    NAME

- _____
- _____
- _____

2 _____
    NAME

- _____
- _____
- _____

3 _____
    NAME

- _____
- _____

From whose point of view will the story be told? _____

When does the story take place? _____

What is the tone of your story? _____

Does your story have a theme? _____

RISING ACTION: Write down your major plot points.

1 _____

2 _____

3 _____

4 _____

5 _____

6 _____

7 _____

CLIMAX: What is the highest point of excitement in your story?

_____

RESOLUTION: What is the outcome?

_____

DENOUMENT: Wrap up your loose ends.

_____

Name of Story: _____

IDEA / INCITING INCIDENT:

You are certain that it's Tuesday, but everyone else seems to think that it's Wednesday. Furthermore, they have never heard of Tuesday!

SETTING Describe three different aspects of the setting.

- _____
- _____
- _____

CHARACTERS: List three characters. Describe each character in three ways. Put a star beside the protagonist's (leading character's) name.

1 _____
    NAME

- _____
- _____
- _____

2 _____
    NAME

- _____
- _____
- _____

3 _____
    NAME

- _____

From whose point of view will the story be told? _____

When does the story take place? _____

What is the tone of your story? _____

Does your story have a theme? _____

RISING ACTION: Write down your major plot points.

1 _____

2 _____

3 _____

4 _____

5 _____

6 _____

7 _____

CLIMAX: What is the highest point of excitement in your story?

_____

RESOLUTION: What is the outcome?

_____

DENOUMENT: Wrap up your loose ends.

_____

Name of Story: _____

IDEA / INCITING INCIDENT:

For a week now, someone has been sneakily following you around, taking your picture and jotting down notes. You don't know why, but today you intend to find out.

SETTING Describe three different aspects of the setting.

- _____

- _____

- _____

CHARACTERS: List three characters. Describe each character in three ways. Put a star beside the protagonist's (leading character's) name.

1 _____
      NAME

- _____

- _____

- _____

2 _____
      NAME

- _____

- _____

- _____

3 _____
      NAME

- _____

- _____

From whose point of view will the story be told? _____

When does the story take place? _____

What is the tone of your story? _____

Does your story have a theme? _____

RISING ACTION: Write down your major plot points.

1 _____

2 _____

3 _____

4 _____

5 _____

6 _____

7 _____

CLIMAX: What is the highest point of excitement in your story?

_____

RESOLUTION: What is the outcome?

_____

DENOUMENT: Wrap up your loose ends.

_____

Name of Story: _____

IDEA / INCITING INCIDENT:

While rummaging around the attic, you discover an old, hand drawn map with a red X.

SETTING Describe three different aspects of the setting.

- _____
- _____
- _____

CHARACTERS: List three characters. Describe each character in three ways. Put a star beside the protagonist's (leading character's) name.

1 _____
NAME
- _____
- _____
- _____

2 _____
NAME
- _____
- _____
- _____

3 _____
NAME
- _____
- _____

From whose point of view will the story be told? _____

When does the story take place? _____

What is the tone of your story? _____

Does your story have a theme? _____

RISING ACTION: Write down your major plot points.

1 _____

2 _____

3 _____

4 _____

5 _____

6 _____

7 _____

CLIMAX: What is the highest point of excitement in your story?

_____

RESOLUTION: What is the outcome?

_____

DENOUMENT: Wrap up your loose ends.

_____

Name of Story: _____

IDEA / INCITING INCIDENT:

Something is just not right about the strange little man that moved in next door. You and your best friend sneak

over there in the middle of the night to spy on him, only to discover that he is an alien, wearing a human costume.

SETTING Describe three different aspects of the setting.

- _____
- _____
- _____

CHARACTERS: List three characters. Describe each character in three ways. Put a star beside the protagonist's (leading character's) name.

1 _____
NAME
- _____
- _____
- _____

2 _____
NAME
- _____
- _____
- _____

3 _____
NAME
- _____
- _____

From whose point of view will the story be told? _____

When does the story take place? _____

What is the tone of your story? _____

Does your story have a theme? _____

RISING ACTION: Write down your major plot points.

1 _____

2 _____

3 _____

4 _____

5 _____

6 _____

7 _____

CLIMAX: What is the highest point of excitement in your story?

_____

RESOLUTION: What is the outcome?

_____

DENOUMENT: Wrap up your loose ends.

_____

Name of Story: _____

IDEA / INCITING INCIDENT:

You find a pair of glasses. When you try them on, you are able to see something that no other human can.

SETTING Describe three different aspects of the setting.

- _____
- _____
- _____

CHARACTERS: List three characters. Describe each character in three ways. Put a star beside the protagonist's (leading character's) name.

1 _____
　　　　NAME

- _____
- _____
- _____

2 _____
　　　　NAME

- _____
- _____
- _____

3 _____
　　　　NAME

- _____
- _____

From whose point of view will the story be told? _____

When does the story take place? _____

What is the tone of your story? _____

Does your story have a theme? _____

RISING ACTION: Write down your major plot points.

1 _____

2 _____

3 _____

4 _____

5 _____

6 _____

7 _____

CLIMAX: What is the highest point of excitement in your story?

_____

RESOLUTION: What is the outcome?

_____

DENOUMENT: Wrap up your loose ends.

_____

Name of Story: _____

IDEA / INCITING INCIDENT:

You find a message in a bottle at the beach. You open it only to find that the writer is desperately searching for

someone... YOU!

SETTING Describe three different aspects of the setting.

- _____
- _____
- _____

CHARACTERS: List three characters. Describe each character in three ways. Put a star beside the protagonist's (leading character's) name.

1 _____
  NAME

- _____
- _____
- _____

2 _____
  NAME

- _____
- _____
- _____

3 _____
  NAME

- _____
- _____

From whose point of view will the story be told? _____

When does the story take place? _____

What is the tone of your story? _____

Does your story have a theme? _____

RISING ACTION: Write down your major plot points.

1 _____

2 _____

3 _____

4 _____

5 _____

6 _____

7 _____

CLIMAX: What is the highest point of excitement in your story?

_____

RESOLUTION: What is the outcome?

_____

DENOUMENT: Wrap up your loose ends.

_____

Name of Story: _____

IDEA / INCITING INCIDENT:

SETTING Describe three different aspects of the setting.

- _____

- _____

- _____

CHARACTERS: List three characters. Describe each character in three ways. Put a star beside the protagonist's (leading character's) name.

1 _____
　　　　NAME

- _____

- _____

- _____

2 _____
　　　　NAME

- _____

- _____

- _____

3 _____
　　　　NAME

- _____

- _____

From whose point of view will the story be told? _____

When does the story take place? _____

What is the tone of your story?

_____

Does your story have a theme?

_____

RISING ACTION: Write down your major plot points.

1 _____

2 _____

3 _____

4 _____

5 _____

6 _____

7 _____

CLIMAX: What is the highest point of excitement in your story?

_____

RESOLUTION: What is the outcome?

_____

DENOUMENT: Wrap up your loose ends.

_____

Name of Story: _____

IDEA / INCITING INCIDENT:

SETTING Describe three different aspects of the setting.

- _____

- _____

- _____

CHARACTERS: List three characters. Describe each character in three ways. Put a star beside the protagonist's (leading character's) name.

1 _____
NAME

- _____

- _____

- _____

2 _____
NAME

- _____

- _____

- _____

3 _____
NAME

- _____

- _____

From whose point of view will the story be told? _____

When does the story take place? _____

What is the tone of your story?

Does your story have a theme?

RISING ACTION: Write down your major plot points.

1

2

3

4

5

6

7

CLIMAX: What is the highest point of excitement in your story?

RESOLUTION: What is the outcome?

DENOUMENT: Wrap up your loose ends.

Name of Story: _____

IDEA / INCITING INCIDENT:

SETTING Describe three different aspects of the setting.

- _____
- _____
- _____

CHARACTERS: List three characters. Describe each character in three ways. Put a star beside the protagonist's (leading character's) name.

1 _____
   NAME

- _____
- _____
- _____

2 _____
   NAME

- _____
- _____
- _____

3 _____
   NAME

- _____
- _____

From whose point of view will the story be told? _____

When does the story take place? _____

What is the tone of your story? _____

Does your story have a theme? _____

RISING ACTION: Write down your major plot points.

1 _____

2 _____

3 _____

4 _____

5 _____

6 _____

7 _____

CLIMAX: What is the highest point of excitement in your story?

_____

RESOLUTION: What is the outcome?

_____

DENOUMENT: Wrap up your loose ends.

_____

Name of Story: _____

IDEA / INCITING INCIDENT:

SETTING Describe three different aspects of the setting.

- _____

- _____

- _____

CHARACTERS: List three characters. Describe each character in three ways. Put a star beside the protagonist's (leading character's) name.

1 _____
    NAME

- _____

- _____

- _____

2 _____
    NAME

- _____

- _____

- _____

3 _____
    NAME

- _____

- _____

From whose point of view will the story be told? _____

When does the story take place? _____

What is the tone of your story? _____

Does your story have a theme? _____

RISING ACTION: Write down your major plot points.

1 _____

2 _____

3 _____

4 _____

5 _____

6 _____

7 _____

CLIMAX: What is the highest point of excitement in your story?

_____

RESOLUTION: What is the outcome?

_____

DENOUMENT: Wrap up your loose ends.

_____

Name of Story: _____

IDEA / INCITING INCIDENT:

SETTING Describe three different aspects of the setting.

- _____

- _____

- _____

CHARACTERS: List three characters. Describe each character in three ways. Put a star beside the protagonist's (leading character's) name.

1 _____
    NAME

- _____
- _____
- _____

2 _____
    NAME

- _____
- _____
- _____

3 _____
    NAME

- _____
- _____

From whose point of view will the story be told? _____

When does the story take place? _____

What is the tone of your story? _____

Does your story have a theme? _____

RISING ACTION: Write down your major plot points.

1 _____

2 _____

3 _____

4 _____

5 _____

6 _____

7 _____

CLIMAX: What is the highest point of excitement in your story?

_____

RESOLUTION: What is the outcome?

_____

DENOUMENT: Wrap up your loose ends.

_____

Name of Story: _____

IDEA / INCITING INCIDENT:

SETTING Describe three different aspects of the setting.

- _____
- _____
- _____

CHARACTERS: List three characters. Describe each character in three ways. Put a star beside the protagonist's (leading character's) name.

1 _____
   NAME
- _____
- _____
- _____

2 _____
   NAME
- _____
- _____
- _____

3 _____
   NAME
- _____
- _____

From whose point of view will the story be told? _____

When does the story take place? _____

What is the tone of your story? _____

Does your story have a theme? _____

RISING ACTION: Write down your major plot points.

1 _____

2 _____

3 _____

4 _____

5 _____

6 _____

7 _____

CLIMAX: What is the highest point of excitement in your story?

_____

RESOLUTION: What is the outcome?

_____

DENOUMENT: Wrap up your loose ends.

_____

Name of Story: _____

IDEA / INCITING INCIDENT:

SETTING Describe three different aspects of the setting.

- _____

- _____

- _____

CHARACTERS: List three characters. Describe each character in three ways. Put a star beside the protagonist's (leading character's) name.

1 _____
     NAME

- _____

- _____

- _____

2 _____
     NAME

- _____

- _____

- _____

3 _____
     NAME

- _____

- _____

From whose point of view will the story be told? _____

When does the story take place? _____

What is the tone of your story? _____

Does your story have a theme? _____

RISING ACTION: Write down your major plot points.

1 _____

2 _____

3 _____

4 _____

5 _____

6 _____

7 _____

CLIMAX: What is the highest point of excitement in your story?

_____

RESOLUTION: What is the outcome?

_____

DENOUMENT: Wrap up your loose ends.

_____

Got a great story to tell?

Have you written a story you are proud of? The author of this book would love to read it. Follow the link to share your story. It might even be published on the Elle Simms website!

http://www.ellesimms.com/share-your-story/

For Girls Who
Enjoy Journaling

http://www.amazon.com/author/ellesimms

Do you like puzzles?

In This Picture is a hidden object book for kids. Each sharply detailed photo contains dozens of hidden images. Some are easy to find and others more difficult. Fun for kids of all ages. Can you spot them all?

http://www.amazon.com/author/ellesimms

Made in the USA
Las Vegas, NV
11 April 2023

70467232R00059